The Hebrew Talisman

By
Richard Harte

Copyright © 2022 Lamp of Trismegistus. All rights reserved. No part of this publication may be reproduced or transmitted in any form or by any means, electronic or mechanical, including photocopying, recording, or by any information storage and retrieval system, without permission in writing from Lamp of Trismegistus. Reviewers may quote brief passages.

ISBN: 978-1-63118-607-3

Esoteric Classics

Other Books in this Series and Related Titles

Aurora of the Philosophers by Paracelsus (978-1-63118-507-6)

Rosicrucian Rules, Secret Signs, Codes and Symbols by various (978-1-63118-488-8)

On the Philadelphian Gold by Philochrysus & Philadelphus (978-1-63118-511-3)

Paracelsus, the Four Elements and Their Spirits by M P Hall (978-1-63118-400-0)

The Stone of the Philosophers by A E Waite (978-1-63118-509-0)

Clairvoyance and Psychic Abilities by A Besant &c (978-1-63118-403-1)

The Rosicrucian Chemical Marriage by Christian Rosenkreuz (978-1-63118-458-1)

The Alchemical Catechism of Paracelsus by Paracelsus (978-1-63118-513-7)

Alchemy in the Nineteenth Century by Helena P. Blavatsky (978-1-63118-446-8)

Rosicrucians and Speculative Masonry in the Seventeenth Century (978-1-63118-489-5)

Qabbalistic Teachings and the Tree of Life by M P Hall (978-1-63118-482-6)

The Sepher Yetzirah and the Qabalah by M P Hall (978-1-63118-481-9)

The Devil in Love by Jacques Cazotte (978–1–63118–499–4)

Fortune-Telling with Dice by Astra Cielo (978-1-63118-466-6)

History, Analysis and Secret Tradition of the Tarot by Hall &c (978-1-63118-445-1)

Crystal Vision Through Crystal Gazing by Frater Achad (978-1-63118-455-0)

The Golden Verses of Pythagoras: Five Translations (978-1-63118-479-6)

Arcane Formulas or Mental Alchemy by W W Atkinson (978-1-63118-459-8)

The Machinery of the Mind by Dion Fortune (978-1-63118-451-2)

The A E Waite Reader: A Selection of Occult Essays (978-1-63118-515-1)

The Leadbeater Reader: A Selection of Occult Essays (978-1-63118-483-3)

Audio versions are also available on Audible, Amazon and Apple

Other Books in this Series and Related Titles

Early Masonic Symbolism by Manly P Hall (978–1–63118–606–6)

Nature Spirits and Elementals by Louise Off (978-1-63118-605-9)

Swedenborg Bifrons by H P Blavatsky (978-1-63118-604-2)

Practical Use of Psychic Powers by C W Leadbeater (978-1-63118-603-5)

Using White & Black Magic by C W Leadbeater (978-1-63118-602-8)

Jesus, the Last Great Initiate by Edouard Schure (978-1-63118-599-1)

Mysterious Wonders of Antiquity by Manly P Hall (978-1-63118-598-4)

Ancient Mysteries and Secret Societies by Manly P Hall (978–1–63118–597–7)

The Zodiac and Its Signs by Manly P Hall (978–1–63118–596–0)

Life and Teachings of Hermes Trismegistus by Manly P Hall (978–1–63118–595–3)

The Secrets of Doctor Taverner by Dion Fortune (978–1–63118–594–6)

Vegetarianism, Theosophy & Occultism by Leadbeater &c (978–1–63118–593–9)

Applied Theosophy by Henry S Olcott (978–1–63118–592–2)

Higher Consciousness by C W Leadbeater (978–1–63118–591–5)

Theories About Reincarnation and Spirits by H P Blavatsky (978–1–63118–590–8)

The Use and Power of Thought by C W Leadbeater (978–1–63118–589–2)

Commentary on the Pymander by G R S Mead (978–1–63118–588–5)

Hypnotism and Mesmerism by Annie Besant (978–1–63118–587–8)

Spirits of Various Kinds by Helena P Blavatsky (978–1–63118–586–1)

The Hidden Language of Symbolism by Annie Besant (978–1–63118–585–4)

Eastern Magic & Western Spiritualism by Henry S Olcott (978–1–63118–584–7)

Audio versions are also available on Audible, Amazon and Apple

Table of Contents

Introduction...7

Preface...9

The Hebrew Talisman...12

INTRODUCTION

The word "esoteric" can be difficult to define. Esotericism in general can be seen less as a system of beliefs and more as a category, which encompasses numerous, different systems of beliefs. It's a bit of juxtaposition, since the word "esoteric" indicates something that few people know about, while the term itself broadly covers numerous philosophies, practices, areas of study and belief systems.

In a greater sense, Esotericism acts as a storehouse for secret knowledge, which is often considered ancient (by *tradition, if not by fact),* passed down from generation to generation, in private. At various times in history, simply possessing the knowledge of some of these subjects, was considered illegal and a jailable offence, if discovered. This usually included such general topics as Alchemy, Pharmacology, Qabalah, Hermeticism, Occultism, Ceremonial Magic, Astrology, Divination, Rosicrucianism and so on. Collectively, these areas of study were often referred to as the esoteric sciences.

Sometimes, the outer garment of a subject isn't esoteric, while what is hidden beneath it, is. As an example, Freemasonry isn't necessarily esoteric by nature (at *least not anymore),* but certain signs, passwords and handshakes given to the candidate during their initiation, are in fact, esoteric, in the sense that they are hidden from the general public.

Today, in the twenty-first century, such topics are readily available at bookstores across the country, and numerous main-steam publishers offer beginners guides and coffee-table volumes on many of these subjects, intended for mass appeal. Books like *"The Secret"* have turned previously arcane topics into household knowledge. All that being the case, however, it isn't to say that there still aren't buried secrets to uncover, ancient wisdom being ignored and forgotten mysteries to be explored. In fact, it is often that we are only able to further our own studies by standing on the shoulders of these disappearing giants.

Lamp of Trismegistus is doing its part to help preserve humanity's esoteric history by making some of these classics available to those students who are seeking to unearth the knowledge of these ancient colossi.

So, be sure to check other titles from our *Esoteric Classics* series, as well as our *Occult Fiction, Theosophical Classics, Foundations of Freemasonry Series, Supernatural Fiction, Paranormal Research Series, Studies in Buddhism* and our *Christian Apocrypha Series.* You can also download the audio versions of most of these titles from Amazon, Apple or Audible, for learning on the go.

PREFACE
By Richard Harte

The present number of the T.P.S. pamphlets, a reprint of a curious and very rare work, may not appear to some readers to have a very direct bearing on theosophical teachings. Those who have got beyond the A B C of Theosophy, however, will find in this issue a good deal of material for serious thought. It deals with one of the most puzzling and deeply interesting problems which the past has left for solution to the future — the destiny of the Jewish race, and the fate of the Holy Land. The *plot* of the work (if that expression be allowed) is based upon two ideas, which taken singly are so well known as to be almost tiresome; namely, the ancient belief of the Jews, based upon prophecy and national pride, that eventually they will recover possession of Judea, and gather together once more at Jerusalem, after their long exile from the land of their ancestors — a belief only less intense than the longing for its realization. The other idea is that contained in the legend of the Wandering Jew — firmly believed in by all Christendom from the apostolic ages until but recently, still half-believed by millions, and to which the doctrine of reincarnation, especially *immediate reincarnation for a specific purpose*, lends, if not plausibility, at least a new intellectual interest. These two ingredients of the plot when put together enter, as it were, into chemical combination, for they give rise to an idea which differs in its characteristics from both of the components. As a punishment for a thoughtless word spoken by a foolish and ignorant mortal even to a god (in disguise at the time), the eternal and miserable activity of the Wandering Jew is a purposeless piece of unworthy revenge, as little credible in this more humane and enlightened age as the miracle required to consummate it. As a practical settlement of the Jewish question, the return of the Hebrew nation, or even a considerable part of the Jews, to Syria seems patently absurd. All travellers describe the Holy Land as barren and poor in the extreme, a land which, if it ever flowed with "milk and honey", has for centuries been believed to have withered under the terrible curse of an angry God. Could anyone but a child imagine for one instant that so thoroughly practical a people as the Jews, a race, moreover, pre-eminently fond of the luxuries of life, would voluntarily abandon the various countries which for centuries have been their homes, abandon their hereditary occupations, abandon civilization, and undertake the frightful labour of reclaiming a rocky and arid district, a labour from which even back-woods pioneers inured to hardship would shrink — and all for a religio-sentimental idea ?

But put these two incredible notions together, and all is changed. What if it be the mission of the so-called Wandering Jew to preserve in the Hebrew mind the recollection of the former glories of the race, and to keep alive the longing once more to revive them ? The moment that idea finds entry to the mind, the legend ceases to be childish, and the longing is no longer unaccountable. The two things explain each other, and taken together they raise the Jewish question to a level far above that occupied by the superstitions of the ignorant, or the calculations of individual self-interest. To the Jew himself it is no less than the finger of Jehovah that becomes manifest from this larger point of view. Through all the centuries, as they believe, He has been disciplining and preparing them for their final triumph. Already the despised outcasts of a thousand years ago are the masters of kings and republics alike. There are a score of Jews today each one of whom is a greater power in the world than an army of a hundred thousand men. Were they to combine they could purchase Palestine ten times over, and then keep a million of Christian workmen joyfully slaving at starvation wages for twenty years in doing the work of making the country once more a garden while they stood by to superintend. Perhaps the Jews are right. It may be that the finger of Jehovah is guiding their destinies in the direction of Jerusalem. We know that to be worshipped there, and by them alone, was once His greatest glory. Far be it from theosophists to deny that such may still be the case, and if it so be, then, for the Jews themselves, all that need be done to complete his purposes will be accomplished. To the theosophist, however, Jerusalem, even Judea, is not the whole of this earth, nor this earth the whole Universe. And a higher guidance than that by human will in the case of the Jews, does not imply a monopoly of divine solicitude for one little tribe of people, nor a monopoly of power and wisdom for the celestial being who has chosen them for his special favour. If it be true that the affairs of the Jewish race are under higher guidance, then logic and justice require us to believe that a similar guidance is vouchsafed to all mankind, and to the inhabitants of the myriad worlds that roll in space. Is it so ? Is there being enacted before our eyes a tremendous drama of creation, in which individual men are as microscopic animalculi ? Does it get rid of the idea of a directing power to call "spontaneous development" what our ancestors, equally ignorant, called Divine Providence ? Who is to ask these questions ? And of whom can they be asked ? Will the Christian listen for their answer from the mouth of a Jew ? Will a theosophist seek it from a theologian ? Will those *who know* go to school to those who invent fables ?

Above, behind, inside of every material thing there is a great, an eternal, incomprehensible, sustaining power — absolute and impersonal, the Divine Spirit. Far lower in the scale of existence there are powers, personal and non-eternal, *creatures* who had a beginning and will have an end. Men call these lower fashioning powers collectively a personal God; not only jumbling them together, but confounding them with the unknowable Absolute. Is one of these minor powers, the Jehovah of the ancient Hebrews, now pulling the wires that attach his people to him, and turning their steps towards the "promised land" once more ? It is said that wealthy Jewish bankers have at this moment actual legal right of possession to Palestine, holding it in mortgage from the Sultan. It is said that Jewish statesmen have arranged for the completion and ratification of the transfer of the property to the mortgagees, upon the fulfilment of certain diplomatic conditions which events are rapidly bringing about. At the present moment a large part of Palestine, and nearly the whole of Jerusalem, is said to be owned by Jews. What does it all mean ?

The T.P.S in republishing this little work, disclaims all political purpose, as needs hardly to be said. It contains some bitter sayings concerning people long since dead, and events now almost "ancient history", all of which the T.P.S. would gladly have omitted in the reprint, had it not been that to do so would have spoiled the consecutiveness of the argument or narrative therein contained.

From internal evidence the Hebrew Talisman was written about 1836. No one ever discovered who the writer was. The edition was soon exhausted, and till now has never been reprinted.

THE HEBREW TALISMAN

It has been lately asserted that so much had been said and sung about the Wandering Jew that nothing further could be made of the subject by any writer, however highly gifted with the quality of invention. Insolent Gentiles! Learn to be more humble in thought and less peremptory in assertion: *I am the Wandering Jew*, I am that doomed one of whom so many have written; and / have smiled in very scorn at the description given of me, and of my mode of being, by personages who are nearly as ignorant of all that relates to me as are those stolid worthies who pronounce me to be a nonentity; and my perpetuated misery a fable and a figment.

I am spoken of as being an undying exception to all human rule; yet has my body died and been consigned to the loathsome vault and the sleek damp worm *upwards of two score* times since that awful day when the veil of the temple was rent in twain, when the earth groaned and was convulsed in her agony of sympathy with the dying one; and when *He*, turning his effulgent orbs in anger upon me exclaimed, "Tarry thou until I come!" Undying! I have been wept over in most of the nations which exist, and in many which have long ceased to be; I have been the victim of the rack and of the block; I have pined in the terrible dungeon of the Inquisition which shuts out hope and which echoes to no sound save the moan of the miserable captive or execration of the brutal gaoler; my body has blazed in the Auto da Fe of Spain and Portugal, where hecatombs of my miserable long suffering race, the youth, the maiden, the matron, the elder, have been immolated; living, burning, sacrifices, offered on the altars of Christian meekness. Undying ! Take but a brief portion of my long and awful history, and put an end to the senseless figments of lively imaginations; to the absurd belief that the mortal portion of man can outlast the rock, and what is frail can remain for long centuries unbroken, or what is destructible remain undestroyed.

-oOo-

Years, long, agonised years, have flown, yet it seems but as yesterday! God! how happy, how haughty in gladness, was I then. My house, overlooking the sea and shaded on the land side by groves of oranges and myrtles, was on an eminence at the extremity of one of the most delightful of the Grecian Isles. Though I was fully twenty years, *in the world's estimation*, what knew the world of my age? — older than my beloved Zoe, I was dear to her as the gushing fountain to the Pilgrim of Zahara. Our daughter, fairest among even the sunny-eyed daughters of Greece, and our son, the noblest boy that ever gave fair promise of heroic manhood, were even as a proverb for beauty, as we ourselves were for prosperity and concord.— Happy days ! Too happy, by far, to be the permanent lot of him who had mocked at the prophet of Calvary, and who has seen empires smitten down, and wept his own repeated ruin in the ruin of successive nations. We sat one evening in luxurious ease, exchanging glances of mingled love and pride, as our beautiful children abandoned themselves to their innocent mirth and displayed some new grace in every new attitude. Of a sudden the air felt leaden in its oppressiveness, a dire consciousness rushed upon my mind, and I once more became aware of my terrible identity. I gasped for breath, and vainly attempted to give utterance to my agony; the metempsychosis of the ancients, fabulous to them, was no longer a fable; and I, who in outward appearance and corporeal members was a merchant of Greece, the husband of a loving wife and the father of beloved children, was once more aroused to the maddening truth, that in soul I was the accursed one of Judea; the survivor of many ages ! the unpitied mourner of innumerable relatives — the dead of divers nations! This fatal, this abhorred, consciousness comes upon my soul in the fortieth year of whatsoever body it inhabits; and to this consciousness some terrible calamity certainly and speedily succeeds.

-oOo-

As I stood with dilated nostrils, glazed eyes, and stricken limbs, my Zoe started suddenly from the anxious and endearing posture she had assumed on witnessing the horrible change which had come over me, and, shrieking, "The Osmanlie!" rushed towards our children. A struggle a piercing shriek, the wild war-cry of the bloody brood of Mahomet; and I was childless and wifeless! How I reached the sea side I know not; but I did reach it and was speedily on board a vessel of my own, and bounding over the blue waters. Days and nights passed by, the good ship cleft her way through the heaving waters; but no pang for wife or child, no thought for my present preservation or future course once crossed my mind. A dry and burning agony oppressed my brain; and but one thought was existent there — my horrible my accursed identity; and when my lips gave utterance to my thoughts their sole accents were "Tarry thou until I come!"

At length this one horror made way for the accumulated reminiscences of eighteen hundred years of misery! Aye, that, that is the surpassing curse of my tremendous doom! No sooner have my forty years of untortured existence passed away, no sooner do I awaken to a consciousness of what I *am*, than I am goaded to despair by distinct and harrowing remembrance of all that I have been, done, and suffered. All who loved me and are lost to me rise up again to my mental view; and the moral evils of long centuries are superadded to the tremendous curse which extends my spiritual evil to the crack of doom.

The good ship bounded on, and the very excess of my misery aroused me to an activity of which I had previously been incapable. Of maritime affairs, I had, in this one of my many lives, had abundant experience; and as the horizon gave tokens of an approaching tempest, I took the helm, and the command of the vessel. If I had not already felt aware that my bodily existence was about to undergo another change, a phenomenon which I now observed would have persuaded me of that fact. Our ship defied alike the wind and the waves, and swept rapidly through the latter in the face of the former ! I then knew that I was approaching my death place; that I was speeding towards land which should afford me another grave, and my spirit, my doomed spirit! another body. Oh, that terrible chill, that paralysis of the heart, that numbing yet agonising sinking of the soul, which precede the mortal pang ! All, all were with me and upon me; yet I gazed in pity upon my devoted crew who, poor fools! were pitting their manhood and their skill against inexorable fate. They knew not, alas!

that to be attached to me was to die; to be bound up with my lot but another phrase for miserably perishing.

Seamen by nature, you insular people are familiar, at least by description, with every phase of ocean's rage and ocean's convulsion. No new description of ship-wreck is necessary to you. Let it suffice then to say that I saw my shipmates, without an exception, swallowed up by the howling waters, and was myself dashed upon the coast which we had long been approaching, and which I had long recognized as the once barbarous land in which, when a Roman centurion, I had combated the fierce and savage inhabitants; and which I had more recently visited as a merchant, and marvelled at for its wealth, its luxuries, and its civilization. Need I name your England.

The valour and the wisdom of their ancestors, had encircled her brows with the diadem of empire and had placed within her hands the Sceptre of maritime dominion, and clasp'd around her waist the golden girdle of the world. She had become the mart of nations, and her ships covered the waters of the globe, and her immense metropolis was the emporium of the earth.

The last fell pang was over, and my spirit once more freed from mortality, to seek another mortal residence. Impelled by the resistless but unseen hand which scourges me, my disembodied spirit glided onward till it reached a small but beautiful cottage, and there at an open casement, it paused; and stood dim, shadowy, and invisible to mortal eye, though silvered and shining in the full calm beams of the moon. In the room sat a young and beautiful woman gazing in agony which *could not* weep, upon the pale and waxen visage of her dead boy — her beautiful, her only one. Anon came the *felt*, though unspoken, fiat; and my spirit entered the lifeless body. The infant's feeble cry, and the mother's shriek of frantic joy announced the reanimation of the mourned one. The father and the domestics rushed in, and the wonderful event is talked of to this hour in the beautiful village of ———.

I have already shown that during the first forty years of each bodily existence, I am unconscious of aught that distinguishes me from the rest of my race. I have but lately been roused from my ignorance: the curse of consciousness came over me ere I wept above the grave of her who had wept her child's death, and knelt in gratitude for his recovery. I am once more alone in the world, and once more aware that I am the accursed one of Judea.

Reader you have seen me though you know it not. A single night has bleached my hair, I wear the haggard features of three score, and as my mean person, and worn yet intelligent features are contrasted, as I pass through the populous streets of your new Babel, with my sordid garments and my anxious and almost ferocious looks, the passengers turn and gaze upon me in wonder, as to my pursuits, my circumstances, and my character.

I am aged; but I cannot again die until my mission be complete. Hitherto, in all my bodily lives I have silently suffered; and in all my bodily deaths I have

"Died, like the wolf, in silence."

But the time has at length come when the cause and the object of my marvellous and doomed existence must be made knovvn; that the pride of the Gentiles may be abated, and that the scattered people of Israel may know that they verily shall be a kingdom mighty to save and to destroy, and that they shall see the advent of *their* Messias, and the utter confusion and abasement of the insolent and false followers of the Nazarine!

"Tarry!" Aye, I have indeed tarried; and I must tarry yet a little while ere the mighty spell can be utterly broken, and the Lion of Judah triumphant over the nations. In what nation have I not lived and suffered? In what nation have I not exerted a mighty, though unseen, power, in producing that gradual rise of my scattered and erring, but still sacred and peculiar, people, which will so shortly terminate in the rebuilding of the Temple of Jerusalem — in the subjection of the Kings of the Gentiles to the sway of the long tried, long suffering, and at length restored, people of the Most High ? The false powers will at length be smitten down by the true; and the temporal triumph of God's chosen people illustrated and consummated by the veritable advent of the veritable Messias. "Tarry!"

Tyrant! I have *tarried*; I have wielded the power of the thousand powers which *may* not resist the word of authority spoken by him who has looked unmoved and unrebuked upon the glories of the Shechinah, who has lifted the veil of the temple, penetrated into the holy of holies, and learned the words of power engraven upon the signet of the master of all wisdom, and of all demons, good and evil — the marvellous, the glorious Solomon.

Ill taught, as are the myriads who put their vain trust in the prophet who died on Calvary, and led away as they are by a thousand vain conceits and cunningly devised fables, even they have some faint understanding of the wisdom of the great Solomon, — whose name be reverenced ! Selah! But they have only a glimmering of light; they can see only an atom of the vast whole of his wisdom and his might; it is needful therefore that they should learn from me what their false philosophy would never teach them, what their false faith shall vainly forbid them to believe. They *must* believe the truth, for it shall chastise them; the word is spoken, Judah shall rejoice over their confusion, yea, Israel shall be very glad.

Though the bigoted and vain Nazarenes know that the great Solomon built to the Most High a temple of exceeding beauty and exceeding costliness, marvellous to think of, though they know that his wisdom filled the nations of the earth with wonder, and caused King Hiram and the Queen of Sheba to look upon him with much reverence; though they know that in wealth, as in wisdom, Solomon was pre-eminent among the mighty ones of the earth, insomuch that none other prince than he could have built that temple, which he dedicated to the worship of the one only God; yet, so narrow-minded and grovelling are these Nazarenes, that they divine not, neither will they confess, that the wealth and power of the great Solomon were but the natural consequence of that ineffable wisdom which was bestowed upon him when his ,soul, in a night dream, replied wisely and worthily to the question that was vouchsafed to him from above.

Nay, so infatuated are they, so surrounded by the outermost gloom of a more than Cimmerian darkness, that they — they! in the petty pride of the ten thousand contradictions which they call philosophy, take upon themselves to deny the interference of the supernal powers in the progress of mundane affairs; though a single glance at their own version of the history of the wise son of David would, one would suppose, suffice to show them that *only by* the aid of those powers, subjected to his unspeakable wisdom, could Solomon have amassed and expended the treasures which upreared the temple. From the cedar that is on Lebanon to the hyssop that groweth upon the wall, Solomon knew the nature and the properties of every thing that springeth up from the pregnant earth; and, divinely taught and divinely authorised, he had elixirs potent for all purposes, and words of might which the demons hear in their far abodes, and which, hearing, they must obey.

As an instance of the unbelieving and deceitful nature of the scribes who from the day of Calvary even to the present hour have laboured in their vocation to hoodwink the worldly and fat-hearted generations, and to keep them unaware of the powers of that magic which, partially revealed to Moses, was entirely unveiled to the steadfast and eagle glance of Solomon, I may demand, who among the multitudinous sects of the Nazarene has any knowledge of that wondrous and invaluable root, BAARA ? That wondrous root which could only be drawn from its parent earth, on being sprinkled with human blood, unless at the expense of the instant death of the animal compelled to draw it ? I venture affirm that not one, save Fabricius, has ever alluded to this wondrous root, except in what the Christians as ignorantly as insolently term " Talmudical fables". And yet it is perfectly true that it is the quality of this root, as is averred by sundry writers of our despised and persecuted race, to cast out evil demons from people possessed; — and, though it is never known to more than one person of our race, a preparation of this root, aided by the words of might engraven upon the signet of Solomon, is potent excedingly in tasking the hidden powers, and in discovering the most hidden things.

Poor fools! these Gentiles! *But* by magic divinely taught and divinely authorised, how deem they that Moses, that mighty chieftain in Israel, foiled the Egyptian Magii at their own weapons, and vexed the land of Egypt with many plagues, even until the peculiar people of God made a glorious Exodus from the land of bondage ? Do they deem that by any other means than magic, so taught, and so authorised, Joshua the son of Nun could have made the sun stand still upon Gibeon, and the moon in the valley of Ajalon?

Touching the root Baara, even the secular learning of the false worshipping people who call themselves Christians, might teach them that its power in the casting out of devils, was well known to our fathers, and demonstrated even to those appointed scourges of Judah, the heathen Romans, whose names be Anathema, Anathema Maranatha. For the priest Eleazer did cast out by its means the demon which had possessed a certain man ; and that the bloody and sagacious Vespasian who was there present when this merciful deed was done, might be convinced that the demon did indeed depart, though the exceeding tenuity of spiritual existences will not allow them to be visible to other eyes, than those from which occult science has removed the scales — the venerable Eleazer commanded that a vessel should be placed at a considerable distance from the person possessed, the which vessel, in obedience to the commands of Eleazer, the demon, in departing did forcibly throw down and empty.

But my proper task will not allow me to bestow further time upon the crude notions or the blind and fanatical bigotry of the detested Nazarenes. The all but omnipotent signet of Solomon *was* deposited by that greatest of earthly princes in the Temple of Jerusalem; and in the Holy of Holies, entered only by the great High Priest, reposed that gem of price and power unspeakable.

When the temple was plundered by the heathen, and when our people were despitefully treated and led into captivity for their sins — the vessels of silver and the vessels of gold were grasped by the unholy hands of the conquering soldiery — Nebuchadonozor and Cyrus bore away the wealth of Jerusalem; but not the signet, which was from the beginning destined to work out the salvation of Judah when her sins should be fully expiated, and her people once more an acceptable people in the sight of the Lord.

But though the dim light of tradition caused every successive high priest carefully to guard against the discovery of the precious treasure, even the high priest knew not *all* the wonders of that treasure. It was reserved for me, the doomed, the mysterious, the ever-changing in body, the unchangeable, the everlasting in spirit, to learn, even while hosts barbaric pressed towards the Holy of Holies, the saving wealth that rested therein. And thus it happened. In the seventieth year after the death of him whom the Nazarenes call Messias, and on the seventeenth day of the month called Panemus, in the Syro-Macedonian tongue, but in the Hebrew Jamuz, the dread enemy of our nation, the Roman Titus had so far reduced the doomed defenders of the Holy City, that the daily sacrifice could no longer be offered; and then knew all those in whom the only true religion had produced the spirit of prophecy that the temple would indeed fall.

I need not recount the horrors of the succeeding days or the siege; or is it not written in the book of the apostate Josephus how the temple was polluted by the blood of our people, shed by each other as well as by the Romans ? How that famine was abroad glaring with fierce eyes, and made horribly visible in gaunt and spectral forms ? How that a mother maddened by famine slew her child, yea, her first-born and her only one, and banquetted in horrible eagerness upon his roasted body ? Alas ! the apostate Jew and divers writers among the Nazarenes, have dilated but too truly and too sufficiently upon the awful scenes that passed in every street, aye, in every house in the devoted city of the living God. Let me then hasten to that concluding scene, which gave the Holy of Holies to the flames; but at the same time gave to me that Talisman, which, eighteen hundred years later, was to rebuild the city and the temples, and prepare the people of God for the dominion of the whole earth, and for the advent of the veritable Messias. Selah ! Let it be done. It is about to be done.

-oOo-

Urged by I know not what divine fury, I had descended from the Upper City, where I had been gazing upon the flaming sword, which illuminated the heavens, even at mid-day. I passed unscathed through the outer court of the temple, now polluted by the bodies of the dying and the dead, and slippery with much blood. Scarcely had I made my way beyond the partition wall, which had been erected for the separation of the Jews from the unbelieving Gentiles; when, from one of the many apartments that were on the north side of the holy house, a lurid pillar of fire suddenly shot upward, and in an instant ten thousand fiery tongues darted from it in every direction, and a cry of horror and alarm arose from ten thousand combatants within and around the temple. To cleave to the earth the destroying Roman, who was in the very act of leaping into the inner court, after snatching from its blaze the torch with which he had now fired the holy house, was but the work of an instant; that done, I pressed forward up the acclivity which led to the altar of Burnt Offering, where the High Priest, who had succeeded the fugitives, Joseph and Jesus, was surrounded by combatants, and in an evident agony of anxiety to make his way into the Holy of Holies. With a loud cry I threw myself forward into the throng and the strife; but though I was swift, I was too tardy to save the venerable man, who, at the very moment that I gained his side, was transfixed by a Roman dart. I raised him and bore him towards the Sanctuary, but though life was fast gushing forth from his ghastly wound, he was a Jewish priest still — true to his God, his faith, and his office. "Pollute not the holy place! Forbear, set me down here, he exclaimed; and in a niche, which was as yet unthreatened by the devouring element, I set him down, and raised his drooping head, and wiped the big damps of death from his lofty brow, all tenderly, as would a nursing mother support and tend a dying child.

His breathing came shorter and shorter, and his limbs became rigid; but the agonies of death had no power over the energies of religion ; and he did not expire till he had commanded me to penetrate the Holy of Holies, and to snatch thence and from the very centre of the ark, the Talisman of our people, even the signet of the wise Solomon — the Shem-ama-phorah.

Not even the behest of the high priest would have caused any other Jew to enter that mysterious and most sacred place. But I! what had I, the wanderer, to fear ?

I passed the brazen pillars, Joachim and Booz, and I reached the golden cherubim, ten cubits in height, whose outspread wings, reaching from the southern wall to the northern wall of the Holy of Holies, had hitherto concealed for ages its sacred mysteries from unpermitted eyes.

I paused, but for a moment; the golden gates were passed, the cherubim no longer hid the ark from my gaze; and, God ! by what a galaxy of glories was I dazzled ! The floor and the walls were of fine gold, glittering with the splendour of ten thousand fires, and reflecting back the many coloured and living lights that flashed from Onyx and from Sapphire; from Chrysolite and from Amethyst; and from every precious stone from every part of the earth. Having drawn aside with resolute hand the embroidered veil of purple and scarlet, behold ! I stood within the Holy of Holies; and there over against the eastern end I beheld an altar of solid and unornamented gold. Upon either side of the altar was a hollow candlestick of gold, adorned with lilies and pomgranates of gems and fretted gold. But *upon* the table! Even I shook in every fibre with much awe, as I looked upon the ark of shittim wood, which in Hebrew is called Eron. It was five spans long by three in height and breadth; and was strongly ornamented with plates of fine gold, and on the top were two cherubims of the like precious material. In that lay the palladium of our people — the seal of Solomon; and I — I ! was to stretch forth my hand and seize it.

The lid of the ark yielded to my mere touch, and mine eyes fell upon the precious signet. It consisted of a single cincture of massive gold, set with a single gem; but *such* a gem. Well might the fiends, well might the powers of earth and hell shrink from the steadfast gaze of its possessor, and busy themselves in doing his behest. In the centre of the gem was engraven the ineffable name of God, and around it in mingled radiance Diamond, of Sapphire, of Ruby, and Emerald, the seeming of ten thousand eyes gleamed with divine ardour to which the lurid lightnings of the stormiest heaven are but as a meteor that dances upon the morass. I stood as one fascinated, terrified, petrified; I would fain have stretched out my hand, but my arm was paralyzed; I would have cried aloud, but my tongue clove to the root of my mouth. As I stood thus entranced a shout in the outer portion of the temple announced the arrival of Titus and his followers. In a few moments the Holy of Holies, the Ark, the very Seal of Solomon, would be bared to the gaze of the profane, violated by the hands of the foeman and the robber. I stretched forth my hand and grasped the signet; a report as of ten thousand thunders shook the whole fabric around me, and I felt myself seized by a giant hand, whose grasp deprived me of my senses at the very moment that I saw the majestic though somewhat corpulent form of Titus within the hitherto sacred place. How long I remained entranced I know not. When I at length awakened to a sense of my situation, I was far, far away from the bloodshed and tumult, from the trampling of the victors, and the passionate but unheeded entreaties of the dying and the captive. The moon, the pale-visaged Astarte of the Phoenicians, was high in heaven, shedding around a flood of silvery light such as she can never bestow upon this land of cloud and fog. I lay beneath a majestic palm, and close beside me gushed a fountain, making a delightful music in the otherwise unbroken silence of the night. It was by slow degrees that all the scenes through which I had so recently passed became clearly and completely recalled to my memory; and, oh God! with what horror did I not thrill when I discovered that the signet of Solomon was no longer in my possession!

I should have raved, Heaven pardon me, I believe I should have blasphemed; but before I could give utterance to my agony, there arose beside me a low, sweet, musical, but withal, most solemn and majestic voice — and the mighty change that had come over my spirit and freed it from the dull and inapprehensive obtuseness of mere mortality, enabled me to know that that voice came from no created mortal. I knew that the voice was a voice from above, and my heart leaped with an exceeding gladness, for I heard much mercy, and was blessed with a most wondrous mission, and with a trust which they who sit upon the blood-stained thrones of the perverted earth might envy — with a power to which they must speedily bow down in humility and in dread.

It was revealed to me that though the curse of him of Nazareth must for a time have power, and though, until the regeneration of our people should be at hand, his power should go on increasing among the nations, the curse his hate and tyranny has laid upon me should be converted into a saving mercy to Israel, a pillar of light to guide and guard the wanderers of Judah. Words of might were graven upon my soul, even the words of the signet of Solomon which all Genii must obey, and I was sent forth to live the bodily life and die the bodily death in divers places; but with ever one task, one trust — to teach the trampled Jew to become very mighty in despoiling his oppressors, very cunning in availing himself of their hearts' leprosy — avarice. Ages upon ages have rolled by; where populous cities and the palaces of kings once stood, the bat and the owl and all obscene and grovelling reptiles are now the sole lords, the sole tenants; and where I have battled with the gaunt wolf, and disputed with the bear his forest haunt, hundreds of thousands of human beings dwell in cities of strength and splendour; the many wearing out their lives in squalor and in toil, that has little recompense and no cessation, the few looking down in insolent and unsparing scorn upon those who starve, that the tyrant and the cheat may fare sumptuously every day. All nations have been in turn the scene of my exertions; all ranks, all pursuits, have in turn been made subservient to the Holy and Appointed end; Jerusalem, Oh beloved Jerusalem, I have toiled to uprear thee in power and in great splendour! The appointed hour is at hand; and then HE cometh, at whose benignant and resistless word the curse of my foe, the fell curse that was pronounced upon me on Calvary, shall be removed, and my spirit shall have rest.

Whether leading the war galley of Venice to the discomfiture and slaughter of the Paynims, or pursuing the business of a merchant in Spain, with the terrors of the Inquisition ever before me, if discovered in my secret practice of the sacred faith of my forefathers; whether passing my youth in the sweet tranquility of an Alpine valley, or amid the roar of waters and the crash of battle; whether in one age wielding the sword and the lance of the condottieri in the cause now of one and now of the other of the venomous little republics of Italy, or in another aiding the revolt of Massaniello at Naples, or catering to the amusements of Louis XIV at Paris; in all times, in all characters, in all places, from the instant that my spirit, *in each new body* has been called anew to self-knowledge, by the sweet low whisper — oh! how full of hope to the Wanderer! — "Tarry thou until I come", all my energies have been devoted to the performance of my task.

The bigotry of a whole people, and the cupidity of their tyrant could easily degrade the Jew in social condition; debar him from this or that privilege, condemn him to this or that burthen, and brand him with an outward and visible token of his debasement; — but the Jew could always amass wealth, preserve wealth, and by his wealth, he, the trampled slave, could always mock the sufferings and sway the fate of the haughtiest and bloodiest of his oppressors. Aye! the Talismanic power has ever been at work; in every land hath its influence at some time been felt, in every land have I at some time made one of my people a mighty man, in the despoiling of the princes and the people who believe in the prophet of Nazareth.

Jehovah! how have I scorned the enemies of thy people, when I have seen them waiting with pallid cheek and downcast eyes for the fiat of the enriched Jew to consign them to instant and utter beggary, or to aid them to struggle on a little longer in the hope of gain to themselves, but in reality only to swell his gains and add to the righteous usury which shall raise up thy peculiar people, and make glorious the towers of Zion.

Alas! how easier far it is to give the Talisman by which riches can be commanded, than it is to inspire a human heart with that intense love of the antique abiding place of our race, which alone can justify me in bestowing the potency and the splendour of riches! How often have I not had to lament the backsliding, and the degenerate self-love of my chosen instruments? With what disgust have I not taken from them their abused trust; with what scorn have I not seen them reduced to despair and self-destruction, by the deprivation of that which I bestowed on them, not for their own petty purposes, but that Israel might be redeemed from her debasement.

Ask who enabled Neckar for a time to support the boundless extravagance of the Court of Louis XVI and Marie Antoinette, and history, the jest book of wise men and the oracle of fools, will tell you that it was his *genius*. I can tell another tale! It was *I*, it was the talismanic power which I gave him for a brief breathing space, to inspire his friends with admiration and his enemies with envy. I withdrew that power, and there arose that scene of bloodshed and confiscation which was especially necessary to enable my people to spoil all the nations of Europe, even as our forefathers by divine commandment did spoil their Egyptian taskmasters. Verily the Jews have had their revenge! From the revolution of

France sprang bloody and expensive wars; from those wars sprang royal indigence and national extremity, which raised up that Christian Moloch of loan jobbery and public debts wherein the present race battens on the spoils and devours the labour of its offspring; and *now, now* was the time when the Jewish people might banquet in the halls of princes, where once their very presence would have been deemed pollution. Now was the time when the aggrandisement of my people could not without sin be neglected. England became the resort of thousands of our oppressed people; and if England insulted and spat upon them in theory, it at least supplied them with wealth boundless and with dupes innumerable. A chieftain of our people became as necessary, then, in England, as formerly in Venice, in Genoa, in Antwerp, in Bruges, or more recently in Paris. From the death of Louis XVI to the consulship of Napoleon Buonaparte, I rarely conferred the visible talisman, for however brief a space of time, upon any one; it was necessary that ALL my people should be up and doing, that each should be amassing his portion; there was a harvest too large for any single reaper; and leaving to themselves the native wit of the Jew and the native propensity of the Gentile to overshoot his mark, by indulging his own bad passions, I looked calmly on, seeing in every bloody battlefield the precursor of a new loan — in every new loan the most perfect of human inventions for the transfer of the wealth of the Gentile to the strong boxes of the Jew.

The result fully justified my reliance on the self-destroying talents of the Nazarenes; the Jews of England amply avenged the Norman atrocities of the older day; and what the Norman took from the Saxons by the stroke of the battle-axe and the broad sword, the Jews now took from the at once insolent and ignorant descendants of those Normans by the stroke of that far mightier weapon — the pen.

The first of my people whom I pitched upon to wield the Talismanic influence in England was one whose name will in an instant be recognized by all the votaries and high priests of Mammon, whether Jew or Christian. I allude to Solomon Salvador. I found him a comparatively poor man; I made him in a brief space the marvel of all who knew him. The wildest speculation he could undertake was sure to prosper; and the magnates of the nation sought his advice when troubled with the common and very painful disease of Impecuniosity.

This success was as brief as it was brilliant. The fool! did he suppose that power was entrusted to him, that wealth was placed within his reach for the bidding, merely that he should call a mountainous mass of brick and mortar after his name, fill it with luxuries from every quarter of the globe, and then spread the banquet and illuminate the saloon to welcome the high-born fool and the high-born harlot, and make glad their hearts with wine and music, while the towers of Jerusalem lay in ruin, and the remnant of our people sat cowering beneath the insolent trampling of the men of blood ? Fool, thrice foolish! I deprived him of the talismanic power, and his wealth melted away from him fast as the snow melts beneath the ardent beams of the sun. His familiar friends saw that he waxed poor, and in the short-sighted wisdom of this world they attributed his downfall to imprudent speculation, to extravagant expenditure, to anything and everything except the true cause; and he died poor, neglected, forgotten.

Possessed of the words of power which the genii must obey, and using those words of power for the great end to which I am ordained, I can convert *any* thing into a talisman omnipotent in the accumulation of wealth for its possessor. The merest trinket, the commonest article of either use or ornament, under the influence of these resistless words, becomes in the hands of its possessor, a weapon mighty as the sceptre of Nisroch.

After I had withdrawn the talisman from Salvador, I cast my eyes about among the young men of Israel, seeking one upon whom I might confer the power which my degenerate protege had proved himself unworthy to be possessed of. Alas ! to find one in all respects worthy of so high and so holy a trust was no light task. Ability, indeed, I found in great abundance among my people: but one was prone to the use of wine, another looked all too fondly on the blue eyes and fair tresses of the daughters of the Gentiles, even of the men whom we call the English; one wasted his time in the light and profane buffooneries of the theatre; while another, though innocent of all these things, though clever, industrious, and frugal, even to parsimony, was wedded to his own base interests, and incapable of casting a thought upon the degradation of his ancient race, or upon the ruin of the city of the temple of God — even Jerusalem.

It chanced that as I on a day took my stand on that grandest of all the money marts of the world, the Exchange of London, my attention was attracted by the saddened yet intelligent aspect of one whom I knew at a glance to be one of our ancient and fallen people, who in the midst of all their degradations cannot lose that peculiar physiognomy which distinguishes them from all other races, and in the very perpetuation of which the Nazarenes, had not God hardened their hearts and deadened their understandings, would see a proof, among many, that the Jewish nation is not wholly cast off, but will, in the good and appointed time, be gathered together from all parts, and reinstated in the sovereignty of Palestine.

Drawing nigh to the person of whom I had thus taken notice, I overheard some few words he interchanged with an acquaintance; and those few words led me to believe that I had at length found the very man I wanted, for he spoke Hebrew with the purity and energy of a high priest of the time when the temple was in its pride of place, and ministered in by the very flower of our people. Moreover, though his aspect had but so lately been saddened and downcast, his eyes now glowed, his mien was erect, his gestures were energetic, and above all, in deciding my opinion in his favour, he cursed the Nazarenes both deeply and bitterly, and vowed to avenge his wrong upon them hereafter. What was that wrong ? Faugh ! What had I to do with the individual wrongs of any one? He hated the Christians, and burned to injure them; *that* was all I cared for; and I vigilantly watched him until, the Exchange closing for the day, he retired to a neighbouring tavern to dine.

What a guttling and guzzling set of swine your mere worldlings are ! A tavern in the good City of London is neither more nor less than a compendious system of damnation; where gluttony and strong wines make sinners of all sorts and size on the six days of the week; their temples, which they call churches, being hermetically sealed to the Nazarenes on every day save the seventh. Gluttony, strong drink, and the sinful thoughts and unclean deeds which they inspire, have the six days — prayer and repentance only one ! Ah ! this is surely a people whom it is especially lawful and praiseworthy to lay under contribution, that the temple may be rebuilt, and that our ancient faith may extend through the whole earth and purify it.

Much as I abhor the devouring and the wassail, which make men to resemble the unclean swine rather than the chief creation and most wonderful masterpiece of God, I sat patiently in this scene of ecstatic and egregious devouring until I found an opportunity to hold converse with the young man upon whom I had fixed my attention. What passed between us it needs not now to particularize; suffice it to say, that on the very next day he netted a hundred thousand pounds, two Christian speculators slew themselves in despair, and ten times that number of the smaller fry took their leave of the Exchange with a very sincere resolution to return to it no more.

For a time my new protege was all that I could desire; but with wealth came luxury, and with luxury come an indifference to the grand object for which I had raised him up from comparative penury; and made him sought, flattered, followed, all but worshipped by the great herd of those who traffic in gain for the sake and for the love of things worldly and perishable.

It was in vain that I urged him, ever and anon, to busy himself for the restoration and the triumph of his long-suffering and widely dispersed people. Pomp and luxury, flattery and ease, had done their work, and *he* too was destined to experience that what the Lord giveth, that also the Lord can take away. Charitable he was, but it was in the wise of the blind Gentiles; looking with dull dead eyes upon the great wrongs and great afflictions of the multitude, and frittering away time, and feeling, and hard gold, upon the petty relief of the petty miseries of individuals.

Charitable ! why Jew and Gentile, the free man and the bond slave, of this most anomalous metropolis of this most anomalous nation, upon the face of God's beautiful, but wrong fraught earth, would shout in contradiction, were I to deny the charity of the great Abraham Goldsmid!

Aye, let the Nazarene dogs lift their hands and eyes in ignorant wonder; the great Goldsmid was my very and mere instrument; I raised him because I deemed him worthy. I found him incompetent to the vast and sacred duty I designed him for, and I dashed him down even as we cast aside the gourd when we no longer require a drinking cup. Who among the elder frequenters of the great temple of mammon, which is called the Exchange, does not remember the golden box with which the hand of Goldsmid was perpetually occupied in his busiest and most important moments? It was his *talisman.*

The words of power had been pronounced above it; with it he could encounter a world and be triumphant; without he was as the stripling David, *without God*, would have been to the giant champion of Philistia. I had warned him again and again; I had menanced, I had entreated, but in vain: I found him incorrigible in his neglect of the cause of our people and our God; and even while he was wassailing at his luxurious villa in the neighbourhood of Morden, the words of power went forth from my lips, and his talisman had departed from him for ever. Large rewards were vainly offered for what all but himself supposed to be a mere toy, a mere thing of effeminate luxury; but those rewards were offered in vain. He appeared upon the Exchange without his palladium; bargained — lost — and saw absolute ruin looking at him with steadfast and unpitying eyes. *Ten days he bore this*, AND THEN BLEW HIS BRAINS OUT! None can be false to our cause and prosper.

The progress of that most marvellous of modern characters Napoleon Buonaparte soon diverted my thoughts from the vexations caused by the folly and consequent ruin of my deceased *protégé*; and hastily leaving England, I arrived at Frankfort just as that city was invested and occupied by the French troops.

I have seen so many towns taken by storm, and, when taken, delivered up to all that the utmost license and cruelty of the most licentious and cruel troops could inflict, and that fate of Frankfort seemed by comparison, to be a mild one. And yet even there I saw enough to make the blood of an ordinary man boil with indignation, or curdle with horror.

With all the politeness of the French as individuals, large bodies of them are usually among the most ferocious of all assemblages. They seem to resemble those chemical substances which, though separately quite harmless, cannot be brought into contact without producing disaster and destruction to every one and every thing in their vicinity. In their revolution I have seen individuals in one hour comporting themselves towards the helpless with all the courage of antique chivalry, and with all the touching delicacy and tenderness of modern politeness; and I have seen those self-same individuals in the next hour hideous with blood, and roaring with stentorian lungs for more victims. Separately good, they no sooner became part of a multitude than the mania of fierceness fell upon their souls, and they became even as the fiends in unsparing cruelty.

-oOo-

What is true of the French people is no less true of the French soldiery, who certainly have never shown *en masse* any of that forbearance which few indeed among them would fail to show as individuals. And if at Frankfort murder, and the other disgusting violence which the conquered sometimes have to endure from the homicidal hirelings, who make a glory and an honour of their most feculent and debased trade in blood; if these were not among the sins to be charged upon the soldiery of France, they amply made up for any inconvenience they experienced from balking their lust and love of bloodshed. It is impossible to conceive anything more complete than the plunder of the unhappy people of Frankfort. Every thing that was portable was carried off; every marauding soldier had his two or three watches; diamonds glittered on the dirty fingers, or still dirtier linen of those ruffians; family plate, consecrated by a thousand tender reminiscences, was melted openly in the streets, and transferred in unsightly lumps to the knapsacks of its new owners. The skill of man was in vain employed to conceal the spoil, the tears and supplications of women were in vain employed to move the spoilers to moderation in their marauding.

The people of Frankfort were a conquered people, the brave French soldiers were conquerors; and though glory, no doubt, is a very fine thing, your thorough soldier enjoys it not a jot the less for being accompanied by a goodly proportion of plunder.

The few people who succeeded in saving some trifling amount of money, were, for the time, scarcely better off than those who were plundered to the very last thaler. For your heroes have prodigious appetites; and the vast consumption of food of every description by the French troops, the terror which kept the country people from bringing their produce into the city, and the blessed propensity of all dealers and shopmen, in all times and countries, to raise their prices in the exact ratio of the wretchedness and suffering of their fellow creatures, speedily reduced five out of every six families in Frankfort to absolute want. In saying this I speak of those ranks of people to whom, previously, want had been utterly unknown, save as a thing which (as their individual disposition chanced to be) they pitied and relieved, or despised and insulted in the persons of their inferiors. Want being thus introduced to homes, where previously it had been unseen and unfelt, it needs no elaborate argument to show that where want had always existed, absolute famine now made its appearance. All trade, save in articles of food, was at a standstill; and at the very moment when the poor were thus cut off from earning the poor pittance to which they had been accustomed, every article of food was tripled, and many articles quadrupled in price.

Fearful, oh ! very fearful, were the scenes which I witnessed during the brief stay of the marauding Gauls in Frankfort. Jew as I am, and detesting, as I do detest, the followers of the Nazarene, with a most holy and fervent detestation, even *I* pitied the unhappy wretches, and relieved their miseries in more instances than I can now look back upon with anything short of the most sovereign contempt for my temporary compassion.

But if I, on some few occasions, tarried by the wayside to relieve some of the more extreme cases of privation and suffering, among the Nazarenes, I was neither forgetful of my proper mission, nor weary in forwarding the great work.

It is well known to all the world that Frankfort has long been the abiding place of not a few of the people of my race; and there are few European cities in which the blessing has more manifestly been bestowed upon their industry and talents. Among the wealthiest of the inhabitants of Frankfort, were certain Jews; I need not add that they were also among the first who were laid under contribution by the unprincipled and avaricious invaders. Finding vast stores of wealth in the possession of some Jews, the French positively, though somewhat illogically, concluded that to be very wealthy was an inseparable consequence of being a Jew, and the whole of our people, even down to those who obtained their daily bread by the lowest toils, and the utmost possible difficulty, were harassed by domiciliary visits — questioned by the officers — insulted, and sometimes even beaten by the men; and, finally, enjoined severally to provide the most preposterous sums of money by a certain given day.

Avoiding, as far as possible, attracting the attention of the tyrants, I passed from house to house, leaving no very large sum of money at any one house at any one time; but taking especial care that however the followers of the Nazarene, because born in different countries, and speaking different tongues, might inflict upon each other the awful agonies attendant upon absolute want of food, no Israelite should lack wherewith to feed himself and his wife, and the little ones that were with them, and the man servant, and the maid servant, and the stranger that was within his gates.

What mattered it that the thaler should be reduced to a tenth part of its value by the abundance of money suddenly brought into circulation by the French marauders, and that the price of every article of food should be multiplied by twenty ? Even then should my people be exempt from absolute famine, — for could I not command gold ? Yea, should the city at length become absolutely destitute of food, had I not the talisman ? — Had I not the ineffable words? — Could I not buy the whole evil race, from the false prophet even to the lowest among the evil genii? — Could I not task them in the midnight incantation, and, lo ! would not plenty make the hearts of my people glad at sunrise ?

So I went from house to house; and while I gave present aid, I spoke words of comfort and encouragement as to the future; and thus from day to to day I visited the houses of the Jews that were in Frankfort. But my motive was not *merely* the desire to afford them temporal aid; contrariwise, while alleviating the temporal sufferings of my people, I was, day by day, scanning the young men with an intelligent and vigilant eye; for where, if not among the shamefully plundered and trampled Hebrews of Frankfort, might I hope to find a zealous hater of the Nazarenes, — a man exceedingly desirous of working their degradation and destruction ? All men are in some sort the creatures and the victims of their own bad passions, even patriotism itself; yea, even religious zeal, to the very verge of ferocious bigotry, can be called into a fiery and active existence by personal wrong, and the personal hate which that infallibly engenders.

An Englishman may read with horror and with detestation the bloodstained records of the bloody and relentless Inquisition of old Spain; but faint, indeed, are his horror and detestation compared to those that tear the heart and madden the brain of him who has seen and *borne* the Inquisition's unimaginable tortures. It is only the wrong which man himself endures that he can thoroughly appreciate; and here, even while want and sorrow were at work, and famine itself but barely kept at arm's length: *here* it was that I might most hopefully seek for a champion to avenge the wrongs of Israel. I sought carefully, and I did not seek in vain; a case soon came to my knowledge which abundantly contained all the elements requisite for my purpose.

Among the number of Israelitish families to which my gold and my sympathy gave me a ready admission and a very glad welcome, there was one to which I was especially attached, both for its own sake and for the sake of associations of eighteen centuries duration. I speak of the family of Solomon De Milheim. If ever modern countenance bore the stamp and impress of our patriarchs of the old time assuredly it was the countenance of the old man, De Milheim; if ever the beauty of the manly youth of Jerusalem, when Jerusalem was happy, was exactly represented in the rising age, it was represented by his sons; and in his daughters the sunny-eyed and ebon-haired maidens of ancient Judah seemed once more to adorn and glorify the earth with their bright presence.

But it was not from such general resemblance that I became so peculiarly attached to this family. Alas ! no; I was drawn thitherward by a most melancholy pleasure; for in the elder daughter of De Milheim I gazed upon the very counterpart of my adored and most lovely Leah — of the stag-eyed wife of my young bosom, whose pure spirit fled the sinful and hard world on the very day on which he, the avenging one of Nazareth, doomed me to long ages of agony and of travail.

It was during one of my visits to the family of De Milheim that I heard of a worthy instrument for upholding and forwarding of my sacred and high cause; and I forthwith departed in quest of him, and speedily reached his abode.

Without, it was dingy, and uninviting as the abodes of even the wealthiest of our persecuted, and therefore politic, people are wont to be; and when I crossed the now unprotected threshold, all within was dismantled and disordered, as formerly it had been sumptuous and tasteful.

Unquestioned and unseen I passed through the various apartments, when on a sudden, just as I had reached the little sanctum of the now solitary tenant of the once crowded house, I heard the clash of arms in the hall beneath; and I had but just time to pronounce the words of great power, which render me invisible to mortal ken, when a French officer passed within a foot of the spot upon which I stood, and threw open the door of the little study with the insolent violence of irresponsible and unprincipled power. As he entered I glided in, and he shut the door as violently as he had opened it.

Seated at an antique writing table was the unhappy master of this desolated house. His eyes were red as with much weeping, and his cheeks were pale and haggard, as with much sorrow and long vigils.

The rude and sudden advent of the Nazarene man of blood and tyranny did not seem to alarm him; it simply and utterly stupefied him. His limbs were stiffened, and his eyes fixed and leaden; and thus he sat, until aroused to consciousness by the martial and haughty tones of the stranger, commanding him to give gold. This demand effectually recalled the scattered senses of the unhappy man.

"God of Abraham, Isaac, and Jacob! " he exclaimed, as, kneeling, he lifted up his trembling hands to the east, "how long, O God! how long ? Have they not desolated thy servant's hearth, carried away his young men captive, and spoiled him even to the last thaler ? Have they not stricken him with many stripes, and cursed him with many curses ? How long, O Lord, how long shall the unbeliever triumph, and thy people be a jest and a bye word, Samsons shorn of their hair, and blind, but without the strength to draw down upon these new Philistines the roofs of their palaces, and crush them in the hour of their tyranny and their scorn? "

"Jew!" said the Nazarene warrior, and the whole fabric shook as he strode across the apartment, "Jew! I am not here to listen to your lying adjurations, I want gold, I will have gold; or, look you, not content with making you as bald and as blind as Samson; by the mother of God, I'll make you as dead as that stalwart worthy! "

"Now, as my soul liveth", replied the Hebrew, "I am spoiled to the last thaler, yea, for this whole day have my lips not tasted of bread, from my sheer and very poverty".

"Bah!" cried the Nazarene, "what be these? Sacre! why they're fine gold and weigh a French pound to a sous!" and so saying, he laid violent hand upon the teraphim, even the images which the heathen of the old day would have termed Lares. In the extremity of his grief, and in the delusive hope that the Nazarene plunderers had paid him their last visit, the unhappy young man of Israel had drawn the teraphim from their secure hiding place, and, lo ! the hand of the spoiler was upon them, and the soul of the young man was bowed down, stricken to the very earth with this consummation of the calamity of his house. It was in vain that the pitiless plunderer blasphemed, and all in vain that he threatened many tortures, and even death; for the young man spoke truly in that he was verily and indeed despoiled of all that remained to him on earth, save the clothes he wore and the dismantled house which he inhabited.

Wearied at length with his unprofitable violence, and perhaps, for a desultory life of war and rapine makes the eye very skilful in discovering between truth and falsehood, convinced by the excess of the young man's agony, that the words which he spake were indeed the words of truth, the Nazarene cursing with many and deep curses, yet looking with no un-pleased eyes upon the golden teraphim which he bore away, departed, and the young man found himself once more alone, and in the solitude of his sorrow he poured forth his unavailing lamentations and cursed the Nazarenes, and prayed in fervent tones that he might have power to crush them, and vowed by the ineffable name of Jehovah to lose no opportunity of despoiling their wealth, and trampling down, yea, utterly bruising, their black and unsparing, as unbelieving hearts.

That was a glad moment to me. I would suffer over again the most bitter misery of the most bitter of any of my many lives to enjoy but once in each day one such rapturous, such exulting moment. Here was a servant fit for the great master — here a champion fit for the great cause. His wrongs, his agony, his fervour, his utter and hopeless poverty; aye, his own passions and his own circumstances would make him a faithful and very zealous foeman to the Nazarene of whatever nation. Here was, at length, the man, the long hoped, the long sought, who should build up the the temple of the Lord, and make Israel and Judah feared and obeyed in all the quarters of the earth.

As the young man prayed to the God of Abraham, and cursed the despoiling and tyrannous followers of the Nazarene, I observed that he kept his eyes constantly fixed upon the niche from which the man of blood had recently drawn the teraphim. Placing myself, therefore, while still invisible, immediately between him and that spot, I spake in my soul the words of power, and lo! on the instant I stood visible before him, tall in stature as Saul when he was singled forth from the young men, but pallid as a corpse, and with hoary hair and beard contrasting with ghastly effect the supernatural glare of great black eyes that shot forth lurid fires upon which no mortal could look and not tremble.

The sudden appearance of such a figure, clad in the flowing robes of the far East, and seeming to spring up from the bowels of the earth, might well appal even the most courageous, and the young man fell down before me, and exclaimed, "As my Lord liveth, his servant is despoiled, yea, utterly undone; as my soul liveth, I have not a coin; yea, even the bonds of parchment which bound many Nazarenes in the power of thy servant, behold, they also are stolen — gone — for ever gone!"

And, as he thus spake, he wrung his hands, and the big drops of perspiration burst forth from his agonized countenance. I raised him from the earth, and spake to him many comfortable words. He proposed to fly from the wretched city, but I forbade him; he spake in hopelessness — and I commanded him to hope; he spake in doubt — and I *compelled* him to believe. I spake the words of power, and the talisman was once more committed to a man of my persecuted race.

It chanced that there lay on the table before him a ring holding the keys of his rifled drawers; and having spoken the words of power, and adjured the demons by the ineffable name, I gave to that ring the influence and the might of the signet of the wise Solomon. Having done this, I commanded the young man to name some wish for instant accomplishment; and ere he had thrice, according to my instructions, whirled round the ring upon his forefinger, steps were heard as of one heavily laden, and I had scarcely become again invisible, when a man carefully disguised, and bearing a large and very heavy bag, laboured slowly and painfully into the room.

"Donner and Blitzen", said the new comer, as he threw down, with a mighty crash as of much gold, the bag he had so sorely travailed under , " I would scarcely play porter again to save my thalers! Time presses, the villains are on the search once more wherever they deem that they have left a coin or a coin's worth. You, I know, are for the present safe, for they are sure you are not worth their time. I know your honesty; and to your biding, until better times come, I commit all the cash I have within fifty leagues, save so much as will prevent the fellows from cutting my throat in sheer disappointment". And having thus spoken, while wiping the big drops from his forehead, he waved his hand and took his departure. The young man opened the bag, counted the several packets it contained and found *the very sum for which he had wished aloud while making his first essay of the power of his talisman.*

Men of the accursed and plundering race! —Ye, whose estates were within a brief space to have been within his grasp; ye whose equipages and whose liveried lacquies I so lately saw following to his premature grave the man of Israel whom I thus enabled to war upon ye in your most vulnerable quarter, — accursed and detested Nazarenes — the young Israelite, to whom I thus committed the Talisman, and who thus early and thus fully experienced its mighty power, — he who for years despoiled you of the gold which you make to yourselves, even as a god — that man whom ye fawned upon, even while you hated him, and knew that he despised you — that man was NATHAN MEYER ROTHSCHILD!

-oOo-

Thus the man Nathan waxed wealthy, more wealthy than any who had gone before him, his riches astonished the gentiles, and very justly they said, such amazing wealth could not be amassed by one man, in so short a time by any human agency, — they were right, it was the agency of the talisman, directed for a high and holy purpose, — to redeem the holy land from the pollution of the infidel, and to raise thy fallen towers, O Zion, from the dust.

Carefully concealing the treasure thus entrusted to him, by burying it beneath a tree in his little garden, while the murderous and plundering French vexed the city with their presence, and using it subsequently for a brief space, with the certain and rapid success ensured to him by the talisman, the young man Rothschild waxed wealthy; and when he had restored the treasure to the prince who had reposed trust in him, he came by my direction, to this paradise of loan-contracting and speculating fools, and became the leviathan of the money markets of Europe. Thus Nathan became the loan contractor, the jobber, the money lender to the gentile kings.

-oOo-

Leaving him to amass wealth, and devoutly praying that he might prove more worthy of the talisman than those who had before held it, I once again made my way to France, for there, too, I had most important work to do in forwarding the great cause.

Superior in other respects to all the men of his time, the Emperor *Napoleon*, so often favoured with what verily seemed to be a fated and inevitable good fortune, was much prone to belief in auguries and tokens, in predictions, and in the whole paraphernalia of the imperfect notions of fatality formed by the Nazarenes of an elder day, and still universally held by the bloody and brutal brood of Mahomet, whose name be anathema!

He held up to the admiration of the French people the phantom of military glory; he played upon their imaginations by the splendours of his intellectual despotism; he displayed the fire of genius and the cool collected judgment of a statesman; and with him seems to repose the secret of governing the restless Gauls.

Availing myself of this, I caused it to be made known, as if by accident; that in the Bois de Boulogne, a man of red skin and horribly huge bulk and tall stature, dressed in the garb of the wandering children of the Arabian deserts, was at times met with by benighted travellers on that road; and that to all whom he met he spake strange words of truth, both in narrating all that they had experienced, and predicting that which was about to come to pass.

The curiosity of the Emperor was excited, and, leaving his capital privately and by night, he repaired to the part of the wood which had been indicated to him, armed, indeed to the teeth, for he was sagacious as the hill fox, but unattended, for he was brave as the Nemaean lion.

That was a fatal interview for him. I found him of this world, worldly; crafty, bold, a lover to intensity of his own nation, a still more intense lover of his own power and his own fame; — all this was well; but so far from deeming the despised and long suffering Jews worthy to build their holy temple and re-establish their antique kingdom, that he, the Nazarene by birth, the infidel by election and in belief, he, HE ! panted to possess and to colonise our Palestine ! I discerned that and he was *doomed*. From that hour he was as virtually lost as was Belshazzar, the King of Chaldea, when the mystic writing gleamed forth, from the walls of the house of wassail and of revelry.

I poured forth into his astonished ear the most secret thoughts of his past life; I ministered to his pride, his ambition, his own impious confidence in his own power, and trust in his own fortune. I became his nightly visitant and his nightly counsellor. The result of my counsels was the march of four hundred thousand of the very flower of the French to attack the Scythian barbarians. Borodino was won; Moscow taken by the Gaul and burned by the patriotism or passion of Rostopschin; the retreat commenced, and — God is great ! — fatigue, famine, and winter, the winter of the North ! did all the rest of the business. Napoleon had accomplished his destiny. Rothschild was right speedily to make that ruin utter and inevitable — not to be repaired.

Though the ruin of Napoleon was decided, and inevitable from the very moment of his determining upon his mad, and thrice madly-timed expedition to Russia, it was by no means expected, or even deemed possible by his supporters, *i.e.*, by nine of every ten of the adult men of France. His marvellous escape amid the hellish fire at the bridge of Lodi; his still more marvellous escape from Egypt, when he sailed through a fog which seemed as if made on purpose to hide him from his fierce and eager foemen of England; these and a thousand other seemingly fated occurrences of good fortune, and, to set aside all the REAL benefits which he conferred upon France, a tithe of which might have upheld the throne of even that honest bigot, Charles X.— his bombastic but felicitous eloquence, and the consummate tact with which he contrived to confirm the French in the notion which they were only too ready to indulge — that every Frenchman was a partner in the glory of Napoleon — made that most *adroit* as well as profound man the very *Mahomet of France*. The followers of the fierce and politic impostor of Araby did not more implicitly and entirely believe in the validity and sanctity of that impostor's pretensions than did the mass of the French people in the certainty, the FATED inevitability, of Napoleon's ultimate success. And, accordingly, the indescribable horrors and waste of blood and treasure at Moscow did not deprive him of their affections; nay, even the treaty of Fontainebleau, which consigned the Emperor to the petty island of Elba, and restored the incapable and gourmand Bourbon to the throne of France, could not abate one jot of heart or hope in the true Buonapartists of France. " He'll return with the violet", was the phrase; and the phrase gave vigour to old men, and increased hope and anticipative exultation to the young men.

  He came, and the throne of France bid fair to be his until his death; by whom was his hope blasted? By the talents of Blucher and Wellington? By the boasted discipline of the Prussians ? By the sheer, brute, dogged, unyielding bull-dogism of the soldiery of England? By the treachery of Grouchy (to whom the *Aide-de-Camp* never delivered the Emperor's order?) By the genius of the allied generals ? By the strength of the allied troops? Not to any one or the other of these did the first warrior and statesman of modern times owe his ruin: but simply Nathan Meyer Rothschild — armed with the talisman !

  The British minister was driven almost to distraction for money; the first houses in London refused to aid him with a shilling. They were doubtful of the success of the allied powers; and the very doubt was within a little of being, like many other auguries, the cause of its own completion, and its own justification. Without money from England, not a small portion of the troops which fought upon the blood-stained plains of Waterloo would have been unable to reach that scene of strife and carnage, in time to take part in the sanguinary business of the three days. This would have been something in favour of the Emperor. But even this was the smallest part of what England's want of money would have achieved in favour of "Le Petit Corporale", *but for the English minister obtaining gold*, THE GENERALS AND THE SENATORS OF FRANCE WOULD HAVE GONE UNBRIBED: THEY WERE bribed, — (to the honour of the frequently shallow and flash, but always honest, Benjamin Constant, I must admit that he, and he *alone*, of all the Chamber of Deputies, refused and scorned the proffered gold); and Napoleon fell a victim to their cupidity. Where did the English minister obtain the means of bribing the constituted authorities of France, and of thus destroying a man, who, but for that bribery, would, to all human seeming, have beaten the armed hosts of his crowned foemen ? There was but one man on earth *who both* COULD and would provide the millions of golden pounds, required for the instant purposes of the English minister. *That man* was ROTHSCHILD. By my instructions he let the Minister have the hard gold; he had my instructions at the same time to do so, only on one condition. Alas ! that he should suppose that a *half* obedience would satisfy me ! As if the wanderer of Jerusalem could know any medium; as if anything could satisfy ME but the full and zealous performance of the Jew's part in the re-establishment of Judah's kingdom — the rebuilding of thy Towers, oh, Jerusalem !

That most elaborate of bad jokes, history, will, no doubt, say that the Jew Rothschild lent the Nazarene elder called Lord Liverpool, the sum necessary to crush Napoleon Buonaparte, in consideration of some such Judean motive as twenty-five per cent, interest. The writers of history, in that case, will, as usual, lie; the readers of it will, as is also usual, be very egregiously and very deservedly deceived. Rothschild was commanded to lend the money on terms very different indeed from exorbitant interest. Nazarenes! those terms were said in a few words! The restoration of Judea to our ancient race; the guarantee of England for the independence of the kingdom of Judea. Ruin stared the English minister in the face if he refused! but he hesitated; Rothschild knew that the minister had already been refused by Barings, Reid and Irving, and all the other chief capitalists, and, therefore, with an expressive sneer advised him to try *them*. The sneer struck home and the minister went to the council. In twelve hours the millions were in the possession of the minister, and a secret agreement, guaranteed by the sign manual of royalty, was in the possession of Rothschild, for the restoration of Judea in twenty-one years from the day on which Napoleon should be finally driven from France. This very year my task should have been completed; *would* have been completed; but he, Rothschild, who for six-and-twenty years had proved himself even as one of the elders in Israel for wisdom and faithfulness, he, HE, at the twelfth hour, proved false, deferred my hope yet once more, and compelled me, all reluctant as I was, to consign him to inevitable ruin of fortune, or to instant exile and speedy death. Though he originally obeyed my behest *au pied de la lettre*, his long round of success (unchecked save once when I reproved his presumption with the loss of a hundred thousand pounds in a single day's business in Spanish Stock, and then restored his lost talisman in such wise as to lead him to suppose he had merely mislaid it), and his profound ignorance of my having the power of, at any instant, recalling the talisman, made him more and more purse proud — more and more utterly and incurably devoted to the art of deluding the Nazarenes, not as a means to a high and hallowed end, but as a source of fortune and power to himself, that it was rather with grief than surprise that I recently heard from his own lips that he had basely sold the agreement for the restoration of Judea for the promise of a petty English Emancipation Bill for our people, and a petty English peerage for himself. This delectable job, this high-minded bargain, was to be completed in the ensuing years by which time the purse-proud, haughty renegade reckoned upon being worth £5,000,000 of money. He was already worth above four; — his *talisman* disappeared, and I took care he should know that it had disappeared *for ever*.

He never ventured upon the Exchange again, or the scribe who wrote his will should have been saved much trouble and time.

Did I give him the talisman, to enable him like Sampson Gideon to intrude his family and found a Peerage among the Normans ? or to stifle his conscience with the weight of riches? or to flatter it with ostentatious charities? No Israelite can put his hand to the plough of this great work, look back and live!

-oOo-

He returned to Germany and was stricken with disease at Frankfort, his recovery precluded, by his *dread* lest my resentment should involve his remaining property. He died within the walls of that very city which had witnessed his dawning fortunes.

For have I not in a nightdream seen Elias? and have I not been commanded to make a new talisman and to bear it to one shown to me and named to me by Elias? and has not this instrument, thus immediately appointed by heaven already made essay of the power of the talisman, and should not the vast fortune of Rothschild have swelled the already numerous triumphs of Israel's new and heaven appointed champion ? Yea, verily.

Accursed Nazarenes ! The issue is now no longer uncertain; even as the stars in their course fought against Sisera, even so henceforth, even until the restoration of Palestine, shall the course of *seemingly* human events fight against and weaken all Nazarene nations, and greatly strengthen and aggrandize my people. In the luxurious and inviting east, in the barbarous and revolting north; among the degenerate dwellers in Italy; among the senseless bigotry of Spain and Portugal; in every land and among every people the Jewish cause shall be unconsciously but potently forwarded; the cause of the Nazarene as unconsciously but as potently beaten backward. Selah, Selah, let it be Jehovah ! THOU hast said it SHALL be.

FINIS.

www.ingramcontent.com/pod-product-compliance
Lightning Source LLC
LaVergne TN
LVHW041502070426
835507LV00009B/752